Out of the Box

Anna Corinne Huffman

I would like to be known
as an intelligent woman,
a courageous woman,
a loving woman,
a woman who teaches
by being.

-Maya Angelou

To every role model,
every friend, and every hero
that has blessed my life with
abundant amounts of inspiration.

Dear phenomenal reader,
First of all, thank you. Thank you.
Thank you! However you ended up
here, thank you. It has been a
bucket list item of mine to write
and publish my own book, and I guess
I'll be able to cross it off the
list now. In a way, this is just a
glorified version of a diary or
journal that has been bound together
and printed out. It's a combination
of random thoughts, semi-eloquent
quotes, and poems that have come to
me. Some pieces in this book truly
required me to focus, sitting at my
desk, writing, erasing, and
rewriting… but the best ones, in my
opinion, are the ones that
interrupted whatever I was working
on at the time. The ones that came
as fleeting thoughts, written on the
nearest surface, whether a napkin or
my hand. I can tell you that,
drawing from inspiration in my life,
there is quite a variety in here,
ranging from enthusiastic to
melancholy and, I think, lots in
between. As I was writing, I
continually was trying to generate a
perfect title for this potpourri of
a book, and then it hit me: *Out of
the Box.* Let me explain. Throughout
my life, people have always told me
to look at the bigger picture…
whether parents, teachers, or

friends. For me, it has always been much easier to pick apart the details in life and analyze them for their flaws, usually with a pro-con list, and while attention to detail is important, overthinking things is wildly unnecessary. At the end of the day, taking a step back to appreciate the masterpiece from a different angle is cathartic and incredibly rewarding.

So… while some of these pages will focus on the details and intricate pieces that life presents, others examine life as a whole. Along with the idea of different viewpoints, getting 'out of your box' means trying something new, which is exactly what it took to create this book and how it ended up in your hands. For a while, I debated whether I really had the drive or the courage to do something like this, and what pushed me to complete it was the realization that I'll be able to look back at this as a mini accomplishment and a milestone in my life. It was nothing but fun to create, and I hope that it resonates with you to some degree.

Lots of love,
Anna Corinne

with old songs and new love
life has provided the essentials.

MIND
YOUR
CONSCIENCE
BE
CONSCIOUS
OF
YOUR
MIND.

she's a jigsaw
with pieces scattered
throughout all seven continents
on a mission to obtain each one.

mentally and emotionally strong people
speak the beauty in others
when they see it.

when you embrace yourself wholeheartedly
each flaw and every feature
it'll become apparent.
a tropical flora blooming
from the depths of your soul
to the tips of your toes.

good things take time
better things never stop
blossoming.

you and I,
we burned with everything we had and
still burned out.

this town is drowning in a sea
of small minds and complacency.

they said she created art
but the truth is
art created her.

they told us Rome wasn't built in a day
but we threw the pieces
together anyway.

when the curtain closes on your life
I hope you feel the impulse to bow
at the masterpiece you've created.

debonair is drawing
which makes him
all the more dangerous.

maybe our grandparents had it better
when happiness was
a drive-in or diner
or handwritten letter.

her life had its own flair about it.

don't allow yourself to judge
another's heart before seeing it
in clear light.
silhouettes only display
a partial image
obscured and incomplete.

I adore travel
with new appreciation
for new places
and new adoration
for the old home
town I love.

being a genuinely good person is worth the while
but wasting time to prove it
is worthless.

love is not
giving pieces of yourself
to fill the cracks of another.
love is
holding their hand
as they find it within themselves
to become whole
no matter the time it takes.

to know her mind
is a labyrinth
of a journey.

this is a gamble he said.
but we clasped our hands together
and with the others,
we tossed the dice
laying it all on the table.

fall in love with yourself
first and foremost.

strong men will love her mind
stronger ones will love
to watch it grow.

create a reality
that is comparable to fiction
by breathing life
into your version of fantasy.

.

she smiled as she walked in the room

and he thought she'd hung up the moon.

you can't save the damsel
who creates her own
distress.

she races down the street
in the black of the night
hair down and spirits up
and the stars sparkle as if to say
when your adventures are complete on earth
come back to us, child.

DEAR LIFE,
TAKE ME TO FOREIGN CITIES
WITH COLORFUL BUILDINGS
AND EVEN MORE
VIBRANT PEOPLE.
THIS LITTLE GREY TOWN
IS A LOT OF THE SAME.

find a love
your five-year-old self
dreamed of
the kind you wished for
when you gazed out the window
of your childhood home
as the stars flew
across the night sky
illuminating the hope
within.

a faith filled life is a fulfilled life.

you grew on me
slowly and miraculously
pushing down the walls
as they crumbled to dust at our feet
an old brick building
and you were the ivy.

each sunrise screams of new possibility.

remain in love
with each breath you've been given
and every chance
that you encounter.

princesses wear gowns and tiaras
queens wear diamonds and bows
and the best of women,
adorned even more marvelously,
wear compassion and grace
with bits of flowers
woven into their souls.

loose lips sink ships
insightful ones will sail them.

they say silence is golden
which would make good
conversation
beyond priceless.

if it's not helping you grow
it's healthy to let go.

if you don't learn how to laugh
at yourself
you're in for a long
and unfulfilling ride.

choose blatant truth
over blind acceptance
they say ignorance is bliss
but in reality
it' s just
foolishness
in a pretty bow tied box.

immeasurable beauty is found
in the souls of those who
have been beaten down
cast aside and
made to feel less than adequate
but maintain hope
scattering a bit of light with each smile.

*conquer inner space
before outer space.*

at the end of the day
the most valuable thing you can have
is an arsenal of good stories
and better people with whom to share them.

down to earth
with a head full of stars.

WITH A BIT OF LUCK
YOU'LL ENCOUNTER SOMEONE SPECIAL
AND YOU'LL JUST KNOW.
IT'S NOT A MATTER OF INTELLECT
BUT A FEELING IN YOUR BONES
ORCHESTRATED BY A FORCE
GREATER THAN YOU COULD IMAGINE.

her life was awfully vanilla
and she dreamed of Italian coffee
French chocolates
and a taste
of foreign love.

people are so much more
than their broken pasts;
allow them
to disprove
your misconceptions and
preconceived ideas.

keep your mind full

and stay mindful.

you can be a realist and a dreamer
with dreams
of improved realities
and realistic ways
to make them so.

lighten up, buttercup
get a new perspective &
a pair of new shoes.

if people are causing you to
question your value
assess their worth
in your life.

in the end, the Romeos of this world are
fundamentally the same
and ultimately dull.
I desire fireworks
the wild spontaneity of a Mercutio,
dependably unpredictable
with wit woven
right into the whole mess.

when you seek shortcuts in life
you end up far more lost than you were
at the start of the path.

the only flawless flowers out there
are the fake
factory made ones
upon the shelves
in the craft stores.

she knew how to play the game,
winning over affection
but losing herself in the process.

please make chivalry
vogue again.

arrogance, the Achilles of the human soul.

in love with the chemistry
of you and me
but the math will never add.

her head spoke a different language than her heart
an energy that fueled her inner storm.

transparency is key
to any good thing
that's how windows
allow the light
to filter in.

*HE REPELLED THE KIND OF WORLD
HE HAD BEEN IMMERSED IN
WITH FORCED CONVERSATION
AND SOCIAL OBLIGATION.*

unoriginality infected
them like a plague
homogenizing
and erasing potential
for individuality.

seek everyday magic
flecks of starlight in smiles
bits of cosmic dust in the veins
of beautiful places
and pure light in the hearts
of the resilient.

satisfaction avoids
the ones who
fail to recognize
their current blessings.

*I refuse to be
a part of mediocrity.*

she was like the sea glass
that drifted to the shore
to suffer ocean currents
and turbulent waves
emerging smoother
than before.

.

my love,
they'd place you in the Louvre
in company
of the greatest of masterpieces
but your wild heart
wouldn't remain still.

self love
she felt victorious in this battle
but knew she fought a war.

I'd describe the feeling of falling
in love
but we humans haven't created
words worthy enough
to encompass the rush
of emotions flooding
every fiber in your body
and pulsing through each nerve
a bit terrifying
but overwhelmingly
and utterly
electrifying.

sunsets are nature's way
of speaking to our souls
with colors that smile
and silent words that say
let today end in serenity
and tomorrow, come what may.

fill your life with color
your home with plants
and your life with beautiful people.

our love is a Cinderella story
fading back to dust each midnight
we continue to strive
for that fairytale ending
but I fear
the shoe will never fit
the way it did in the storybook.

fall head over heels in love
with new towns
far more often than with people.

her heart was a blooming Eden
but hidden behind a wall of thorns
because no one had taught her
strength and vulnerability
could coexist.

there are too many people
playing games
these days
with facades and charades
and masquerades.

strong willed
and grace filled.

the greatest superpower one can possess
is the ability to maintain
a fine balance between
self love and selflessness.

your laughter makes the stars dance
in little whirls
they float around in the universe
at the joy of your heart.

the way he enchanted the air
made all commonplace things burst alive
bringing vibrancy to even the greys.

life is a boundless maze of trails with no map or compass to guide us. all we possess on our journey is a little faith and lots of love. love from ourselves, love from others, and love from God. life can be a spontaneous adventure with friends. it can be views from the mountaintop or sights below waters. it can be early morning coffee or late-night stargazing. it can be long evening car rides with the windows rolled down or stormy November days with a good book. it can be laughter and peacefulness, hard work and carefree moments, silly and serious, and every piece in between. it can be heartbreaking at times, but those feelings can be overcome by the love of the ones around you and the love you hold for yourself. it can be the most adventurous life you make it, and the path you choose is yours to walk, but you can always bring along a friend. life can be amazing, with each day holding its own opportunities, memories, and lessons. life can be everything you dreamed it could be, and much, much more. life can allow memories to bloom, relationships to flourish, and knowledge to grow. the only things life requires of you in exchange for her bountiful gifts, is an open heart and a faithful spirit. it's all in your hands.

eyes speak the truth
even when tongue, when lips
when voice
don't.

love radiated through her.
pulsing through her veins
it shone from her smile
as beams of light,
emerging from her fingertips.
each joyous tear watered
little yellow dandelions.

building a future

doesn't require you

to tear down the past.

he's the sun
before the burn.

she had a beautiful life
but tainted it with her incessant worry
and unnecessary perfectionism.

it's the stories like ours
that end up on the silver screen.

we've been down this road
a multitude of times
and nothing seems to change.
we both grow,
just not together.

after months of crossed wires
and housefires
we inevitably went up
in columns of smoke
and a little pile of ash
is all that remains
on the dusty linoleum
kitchen floor.

perhaps life's greatest challenge is to find
the wild inside our souls and
the practicality inside our minds
and to maintain balance
with a little more wild than not.

anonymity is often beautiful and
rock bottom highlights potential.

gardening is simple; pull the weeds
keep the flowers.
people are more challenging
we're all a bit weed and a bit bloom
a little messy, a little breathtaking.

life's immeasurably more exquisite
when you choose to chase sunsets
and other far off things.

it's a good life
when all is said and done.

time will weather our love
until we erode and blow
to the winds.

gravitate towards people
who aren't intimidated by
your intelligence or power.

stand by the people whose hearts
cast sun rays upon yours.

it's heartbreaking to watch
people sitting around
waiting
for an invitation
to their own lives.

for you, my dear,
I'd rehang every star
but the most gorgeous ones
are in your eyes.

aspire to be like the daisies
that grow through the cracks
of the pavement
to resist limitations
to spread beauty despite all things.

the best moments in life
are the ones you don't spend
abundant amounts of time
and inordinate amounts of money on.

live for the serendipitous

pursue spontaneity.

her biggest fault was her failure
to recognize the beauty shining through her
like beams of light that
stretched
from the inner corners of her soul.
she was earth's second sun.

being alone should never be lonely
when done correctly
for you are your best company
and longest commitment.

live music is for the truly living.

to all the gals out there in this world, you are worthy. you are worthy of every happiness, of every laugh, and of every bit of sunshine you encounter. you deserve to fall in love, learn from it, and learn to love again. your beautiful brain is intelligent enough to become anything you want to become, and you hold every piece of potential at the tips of your fingers. life is an open road for you to experience. you can choose to travel the world, get married, have a child, or five, get a dog, and do whatever. you. want. if that doesn't encourage you, just think, this life is a temporary one hundred years, and after that, you will be reunited with the one who created you, loved you more than anyone could, and saved you. He created every single one of your unique and beautiful features, and to feel anything less than adequate is to feel ashamed of God's work, and He wants you to embrace yourself wholeheartedly. the beauty in that alone should encourage you to love yourself, every flaw and mistake you've made, not because they taint you or make you imperfect, but because they make you human, and that's a beautiful thing to be.

*she was a classic girl
in a fast-paced world.*

set life at a good pace
fly away to a new place
make time for your headspace.

he reached his hand towards
mine
and for a split second
I found my Eden in this broken world.

I see your face in every stranger
a terrible and lonely curse
but I wouldn't wish away the pain
because it's proof of the passion
a wildfire
that existed
once upon a time.

there are no Prince Charmings
in this world
just a few people
who will adore your quirks
find beauty engrained
in your flaws
and these are the ones
you want to hold on to.

you gifted me immeasurably
and I have devoted myself to you
as the flowers turn
with a smile
to face their sun.

humble yourself to life's lessons
she's far wiser than you.

my love,
  I'd bottle each star and every sunset for you
but beauty like that cannot be contained
you're living proof.

she had flecks of gold in her eyes
and freckles on her nose
as her sunshine
soul burst through
in subtle
but remarkable
ways.

the earth has gifted us
this broken road
can be our home
as long as the sun continues
to reign in her sky
and the heavens smile upon us.

if mountaintops were simple to reach
they'd be far less spectacular.

her curious mind craves answers
after sundown and before sunrise
sleep seems trivial
when there is so much to discover.

she has a twenty-four-carat mind
and a heart embedded with diamonds.

toss pennies into fountains
to become a bit richer.

love purely
or she'll show you why
they name hurricanes
after women like her.

true love

or truly loving someone

are two very different things

one exists

the other is perceived.

falling in love with you
meant falling out of love
with myself.

our love language was the same

but the dialect was off.

evenings should be nothing short
of good music and bonfires.

gratitude
will always be the ultimate
and quickest acting antidote
for a variety of ills.

I thought it was remarkable
how she seemed to lose herself
in her book
in reality
she was finding herself.

it's the promise of sunny days
that make the ones like these
worth all the while.

she's a little bit girl next door
a little bit lioness.

it's not about your capacity for intellect
it's about your capability for empathy.

GOD IS THE ULTIMATE ARTIST
FOR HE DREW UP THE SEA AND
PAINTED THE SKY TO MEET IT
WITH A SUN TO KISS
THE EARTH AWAKE EACH MORNING
AND THE STARS TO SING
HER A LULLABY
EACH NIGHT.

*love creates the worst forms of
withdrawals in people
as loss creates
torrential downpour and
thunderous crashing
as the heart collides and
flakes apart.*

wish upon a star

then fly up to join it.

nostalgia can be a beautiful thing
connecting us to the past
but suffocating
if we hold on too tight.

it can be rocky
and yet
still marvelously
captivating.
–　Washington beaches

the most resilient

and intriguing people

have walked an old dusty road

experienced shattered hearts

crossed broken bridges

burned them to ash

and still exemplify strength

despite it all.

*when you're lying
on your death bed
you'll regret
not kissing the girl
in the rain.*

she had so much love inside
but saved none for herself.

he said he had to leave me
to see the world
which left me broken
because he was mine.

we were suspended
in midair
knowing gravity would pull us back
down
but we chose naiveté instead
a foolish and temporary compromise.

SHE PAINTED OVER HER SCARS
WITH PLATINUM AND SELF
CONFIDENCE.

running to you was a childish mistake
a kid dashing to freshly fallen snow;
beautiful
but chilling to the bone.

every time he smiles

the sun darkens in comparison.

as they ran outside
they taught the forest
what it meant to be
wild
even the wolves looked upon them
with envy.

our souls are linked
through hell or highwater
if it's hell, we'll burn
brighter
if it's water, we'll climb
higher.

with you
each day is a trip
down the rabbit hole
and straight into madness.
a bit off with your head
for we have both lost our minds
as the tables flip midair
vases of painted roses
dripping red
crash against the wall
with swords in arms
we continue to fall.

unwonderful wonderland

even a star collapses

in on itself

a bit

before creating its supernova.

the women who are a force of nature
are to be feared and respected
a tsunami
and the eye of a storm
swirling in order
and disarray.

she says she wants to change the world
but fears to change her own.

forever in love with
the instant euphoria
of stepping off a plane.

like the rings of Saturn
I desire to surround you
devoted
eons from now.

his soul was corroded into bits of cosmic dust.

we are born with a primal desire
to seek love and adventures,
leave this life in the same manner.

life hardened her
inured and jaded
a heartbreaking thing
to view.

the best days consist of
a tank of gas
a book of maps
and a mind to clear.

she spoke with eloquence and grace
alluring like a siren
with a penetrating gaze.

to combine the intensity of his eyes
with the rhythm of his heart
is to bottle my own personal elixir
an aphrodisiac in a little glass vial.

no matter how far
you wander this earth
I'll cherish your heart
and all of its worth.

these days,
life has been full of decisions
like balancing
on a cliff
the precipice of safety
and infinite 'what ifs'
the water below screams of adventure
but the fall could be home to numerous dangers
and it's this ultimate
ultimatum
that keeps many people safe
high and dry
with the freedom to fly
though never truly alive.

you'll give me safety
and I'll give you freedom.
together
we'll float up to the stars each night
and return to earth
when the sun starts to rise.

as children
we wished on stars
and trips to Neverland
but the magic was always
at the tips of our hands.

you'll rarely make an impact
if your heart isn't involved.

forever dancing the line
of love and hate
for that bittersweet feeling
of living a moment
that already feels like a memory
when perfection surrounds
and the stars align
but the sun will rise
and this momentary blip
will live on
only in my mind.
memories to fade
with the weathering of time.

with the elegance of Hepburn
the allure of Monroe
& the innovation of Chanel.

*the best mornings consist of
indie music and
coffee with whipped cream.*

there is a myriad
of spectacular things
to experience in life
none of which include
dead end careers and
unfulfilling relationships.

when you fall in love with a firework
you can expect to be burned.

they say tropical flowers

are unable to bloom

in Washington

clearly, they failed

to account for you.

the only things that connected
the people
in that cold, grey town
were the telephone lines
and rusted street signs.

love is a language we all
possess the capability
to speak
with eloquence and flair
but for most
we spend our whole lives
working to achieve
fluency.

country music
genuine smiles and
love letters are timeless
art forms
that continue to be fewer

and

farther

between.

leave the vivacious girls
for the shyest guys
with a bit too much
grey melancholy
hidden within their eyes.

hey birth mother,
I am complete
I am beyond whole
I'm strong and loud
unapologetically proud
of the woman I am becoming.
I have a beautiful world
was a happy little girl
but that doesn't prevent me from wondering:

do my eyes shine like yours
do you have kids you adore
do you sleep in a bed
or a cold, wooden floor
do you have a husband you love
with a heart that is full of
gold and passion- do you fight
when push comes to shove?

no matter the answer
I continue to thrive
I wish you health and
I'm keeping your memory alive
you gave me this life
and with all of my heart
I've honored your choice
and my life's become art.

your attraction was magnetizing
spinning my inner compass
away from the original direction.

I held his hand tightly
with the hope that colors from his soul
would somehow seep into mine.

God blesses
everyday heroes
and hometown miracles.

an ego has no place
in the decision-making
process.

all the love to
the teachers
whose lessons extended
far beyond the scope
of a textbook.

fate's ability to place
the right people
in the correct place
at the proper time
is astounding.

constancy is comfortable
but seasons bring about new
growth.

sometimes I want

a simple white picket fence life

other times, I'd sell it

all for the possibility

of setting the world on fire

even for a second.

life extends a hand
to those who push their minds
out of the box
of normality
and into a new realm
of possibility.

the richest man on earth
doesn't line his pockets with coins
but his life
with intangible gems.

I escaped the tower and slayed my own dragons
realizing my fate was always mine to make
and the game changed.

she was broken
in all her magnificence
a fallen star,
but his sun.

self-love is a living
organism
in need of
sunlight and water
each day.
a little love here
a bit of laughter there.

fully convinced
that the sassier girls
live a bit longer,
and if not,
at least they live better.

THEY SAID TO CHASE DREAMS
NOT PEOPLE
BUT WITH YOU,
THEY'RE ONE AND THE SAME.

used bookshops
contain a bit of magic
among the shelves
each book contains a story
within them
and each has been a part
of someone else's story
for a time.

I would have walked this tightrope
with you
to the end of the line
but the rope was frayed
from the start.

she was so scared
of losing him
that she lost herself
a far more
frightening reality.

unspoken words become

reams

of

paper

scenarios in the mind

and

infinite

*why*s and *what if*s.

that vibration in your chest
you feel
when you enter a new town
means you'll discover a little
piece of yourself among
the coffee shops and hanging baskets.

he's my sun
I will orbit all my days
hoping gravity will pull us in
to burn brighter together.

the gift of living in Bellingham
is a taste for incomparable coffee
and forests
unparalleled in beauty.

the more you throw upon her
the more she burns
her soul is fire
and thirsts
for the fuel of challenge.

glass can be stained and become even lovelier;

so, too, can you.

place good into the universe

and good shall find its way back

just as the sea reflects the sun's light each day.

to the women
who have taught the girls
what it means to fill their hearts
with adoration for themselves and
others
the earth spins for you
and by you.

it's going to be a lonely road
if you don't want to spend the rest
of your life
with yourself first.

let your tears fall
take a lesson from the clouds
and release
what you've been holding.
by way of rain or thunder.
catharsis is essential
for a clear mind
and the storm will pass
it's a matter of time.

when someone you believe in
disappoints
it's like waking up to realize
you planted seeds of hope
in a graveyard
instead of a garden.

the farther the roots
the worldlier the person
and the deeper their
knowledge runs.

she's in love with cities she has never seen
nostalgic for a time she has never known.

*if someone wants
to leave,
allow them to do so
and begin to heal.
you deserve more
than a half-devoted heart.*

DON'T
TRUST
PEOPLE
WHO
DRIVE
WITH
THEIR
WINDOWS
UP
ON
SUMMER
NIGHTS.

I'm a bit of a contradiction
but that's okay
even the trees stretch to the heavens
while remaining rooted
in the ground.

understand the difference
between guarding your heart
and sealing it off.
self preservation not deprivation.

I finally figured out
it's perfectly acceptable
to not have it figured out
and was able to breathe
for the first time in years.

new cities mean
phenomenal street art
and a fresh beating heart.

being human being can be
an overwhelming
and underappreciated thing.

you played a good game
but in the end,
I was just a pawn
to remove from the board
before you took
your queen.

her soul is marked by the ones who have
loved her
tattoos of adoration
she wears on her conscience with pride.

when she sings
angels smile from the clouds
words dance off her tongue
into the hearts of those near.

I'd rather spend my precious
and valuable time
surrounded by women
with blossoming minds.

opportunities flow by
you can't touch the same
river water twice.

we drive
to keep up with our thoughts
racing through the night
speeding down the street
flying with light.

the most devastating thing
is the feeling of losing someone
without a method of prevention
like trying to hold light
or watching sand
slip through
your fingers.

sometimes it feels
like Halloween
every day in this town
with masks and secrets
left to be found.

why do we so easily build barriers
divide lands
and cast away others
when the same earth feeds us
the same sun warms us
and the same moon
watches over us each night.

the best smiles take over the body
and its entirety
as joy overwhelms
and happiness bursts through.

your worth far exceeds
what you have been made to believe.

the most intriguing
women
with the best stories
and intoxicating laughs
have taken life
and lived it to the hilt.

autumn is a magnificent time

the leaves know their season is ending

but fall with grace

and burning color.

don't bargain away your
happiness
for the presence of others.

standing above a city at night
is a juxtaposed flood of emotions.
with millions of people
below for miles
loneliness comes in waves
but in the silence
your problems dissolve
and float to the stars
and it's the realization that you're
a piece of a buzzing hive of life
a network of streets and heartbeats
you're a part of something grand
where minor things dissipate
and how can your soul not glow
at something as marvelous
as that.

the best people
don't alter others.
rather, they remind them
of the hidden jewels they always possessed
within them from the start.

☆ ☆

stars

the ☆

to

on a stairway up

collecting memories

along the way.

with all my love,
I wish you venturesome days
and halcyon nights.

the best music out there

- Old Pine / **Ben Howard**
- Portugal / **Walk the Moon**
- Let's Hurt Tonight / **One Republic**
- Wish I Knew You / **The Revivalists**
- House of Gold / **Twenty-One Pilots**
- Awake My Soul / **Mumford & Sons**
- Geronimo / **Sheppard**
- Love Lies / **Khalid**
- Hard Love / **NEEDTOBREATHE**
- Ophelia / **The Lumineers**
- Someone New / **Hozier**
- Take it All Back /**Judah & the Lion**
- Good Grief / **Bastille**
- Way Down We Go / **Kaleo**
- Stole the Show / **Kygo**
- Every Day's the Weekend / **Alex Lahey**
- Mess Around / **Cage the Elephant**
- Baseball / **Hippo Campus**
- Hold Back the River / **James Bay**
- Waste a Moment / **Kings of Leon**
- Say Something Loving / **The xx**
- Saturday Sun / **Vance Joy**
- First / **Cold War Kids**
- Walk the Line / **Johnny Cash**
- Somebody / **The Chainsmokers**
- Help Me Run Away / **St. Lucia**
- Young and Beautiful / **Lana Del Rey**
- Happy Accidents / **Saint Motel**
- She's Out of Her Mind / **Blink-182**
- Tokyo Sunrise / **LP**
- High Dive / **Andrew McMahon in the Wilderness**
- Everybody Lost Somebody / **Bleachers**
- Unbelievers / **Vampire Weekend**
- Mountain Sound / **Of Monsters and Men**

- Tongue Tied / **Grouplove**
- Save Rock and Roll / **Fall Out Boy**
- Smile / **Mikky Ekko**
- The Night We Met / **Lord Huron**
- Renegades / **X Ambassadors**
- Meaning of Life / **Kelly Clarkson**
- All We Ever Knew / **The Head and the Heart**
- Silhouettes / **Colony House**
- She Is / **Ben Rector**
- Life Changes / **Thomas Rhett**
- Take Me Home / **Jess Glynne**
- My Body / **Young the Giant**
- LA Devotee / **Panic! at the Disco**
- Walking in Memphis / **Marc Cohn**
- Lost Boy / **Ruth B**
- Budapest / **George Ezra**
- Reflecting Light / **Sam Phillips**
- Sober Up / **AJR**
- Hold On / **Chord Overstreet**
- Never Going Back Again / **Fleetwood Mac**
- Naked as We Came / **Iron & Wine**
- Begging for Thread / **Banks**
- 7 Years / **Lukas Graham**
- Hallelujah / **Jeff Buckley**
- Glitter and Gold / **Barns Courtney**
- S.O.S / **ABBA**
- Love You Like That / **Dagny**
- Made to Find You / **Belle Mt**
- Dog Days Are Over / **Florence + the Machine**
- Human / **Rag'n'Bone Man**
- Battleships / **Daughtry**
- Supermarket Flowers / **Ed Sheeran**
- Same Old Blues / **Phantogram**
- Spirits / **The Strumbellas**
- Gone, Gone, Gone / **Phillip Phillips**
- Hold You in My Arms / **Ray LaMontagne**

Luke 1:45

Anna Corinne is a high school student
in Washington state, near the beautiful
Bellingham area aka 'the city of
subdued excitement'. She thoroughly
enjoys alternative music, her dog,
traveling to new places, exploring the
ones nearby, and spending time with her
friends and family. She is a music
lover, Christmas adorer, autumn
enthuser, and avid shoe buyer. As far
as the future goes, she will be
finishing high school, attending
university in a few years, and beyond
that, it is yet to be written.